Greatest Moments in BYU Sports History

Dr. Robert H. Stauffer Jr.

Published by Robert Stauffer, 2024.

While every precaution has been taken in the preparation of this book, the publisher assumes no responsibility for errors or omissions, or for damages resulting from the use of the information contained herein.

GREATEST MOMENTS IN BYU SPORTS HISTORY

First edition. September 26, 2024.

Copyright © 2024 Dr. Robert H. Stauffer Jr..

ISBN: 979-8224264278

Written by Dr. Robert H. Stauffer Jr..

Table of Contents

Celebrating the Legacy of BYU Sports

The journey through the storied history of Brigham Young University (BYU) sports is a testament to the power of perseverance, excellence, and the relentless pursuit of greatness. Over the decades, BYU has carved out a niche for itself not only in the hearts of its passionate fans but also in the annals of collegiate athletics. From thrilling victories on the football field to heart-stopping moments on the basketball court, BYU sports have provided countless memories that resonate with students, alumni, and supporters alike. This book aims to celebrate the greatest moments in BYU sports history, highlighting the unforgettable events that showcase the university's rich athletic legacy. As we delve into these iconic moments, it becomes clear that BYU's success is rooted in a culture that emphasizes hard work, dedication, and a commitment to excellence. The foundation of this culture was laid in the early years, where determination and grit propelled athletes to push beyond their limits. BYU's unique environment, influenced by the values of the Church of Jesus Christ of Latter-day Saints, has cultivated a spirit of community and support, fostering athletes who strive not only for personal glory but also for the pride of their university and the greater good of their community.

Among the highlights that define BYU's athletic heritage is the 1984 football national championship, where the Cougars triumphed over Michigan in a nail-biting Holiday Bowl showdown. This remarkable feat remains a cornerstone of BYU's football narrative and is emblematic of the team's tenacity and resilience. Similarly, the 1980 Miracle Bowl, where BYU mounted an astonishing comeback against SMU, exemplifies the unyielding spirit of Cougar athletes, capturing the essence of what it means to never give up. These moments, among many others, form a tapestry of triumphs that paint a vivid picture of BYU's journey through the world of sports.

Athletes like Ty Detmer, Jimmer Fredette, and Steve Young have left indelible marks on the university, each contributing to BYU's rich sports legacy. Detmer's Heisman Trophy victory in 1990, Fredette's incredible scoring prowess, and Young's remarkable journey from a college standout to a Hall of Fame NFL quarterback exemplify the talent and determination found within BYU's ranks. Their stories inspire not only future athletes but also anyone striving to achieve greatness in their pursuits.

Furthermore, BYU's achievements are not limited to football and basketball. The university has made significant strides across various sports, including women's soccer, volleyball, and rugby, showcasing the depth of talent within its athletic programs. Each championship, record, and memorable play adds to the university's rich sports history, illustrating that the Cougar spirit thrives in diverse arenas.

As we turn the pages of this book, we invite you to relive these unforgettable moments that have shaped BYU sports and inspired generations. Each chapter will take you on a journey through time, providing insights into the athletes, coaches, and games that have defined this proud institution. From historic victories to personal milestones, the stories within these pages will resonate with anyone who has ever donned a BYU jersey or cheered from the stands.

In celebrating these moments, we not only honor the past but also look toward the future, acknowledging that the legacy of BYU sports will continue to grow as new athletes rise to the challenge and create their own unforgettable memories. This is more than just a recounting of moments; it is a celebration of a community, a culture, and an unwavering commitment to excellence that defines BYU sports. Let us embark on this journey together, reliving the thrilling highs and poignant lows that have shaped the legacy of BYU athletics, as we pay tribute to the greatest moments in Cougar history.

1951 NIT (National Invitation Tournament) Basketball Championship

In 1951, the BYU men's basketball team achieved a historic milestone by winning the National Invitation Tournament (NIT) championship. At that time, the NIT was considered one of the premier postseason tournaments, rivaling the NCAA Tournament in prestige.

Key Details of the Championship:

- Tournament Journey: BYU's path to the championship was marked by impressive victories over formidable opponents. The Cougars showcased their talent and teamwork throughout the tournament, culminating in a thrilling final.

- Final Game: The championship game was held at Madison Square Garden in New York City, a prestigious venue for college basketball. BYU faced Duke in the final, winning the game 79-73 in a tightly contested matchup.

- Star Players:

  o Mel Hutchins, who was instrumental in the victory, was recognized for his outstanding performance throughout the tournament. His scoring and rebounding were key to BYU's success.

  o Clyde B. Smith also played a crucial role, contributing significant points and helping to lead the team.

Historical Significance:

- First Major Title: The 1951 NIT championship marked BYU's first major national title in basketball, elevating the program's status and showcasing its competitiveness on a national stage.

- Legacy: Winning the NIT helped establish BYU as a significant player in college basketball and paved the way for future successes. The championship also contributed to the growth of the program and the popularity of basketball at BYU.

THE 1951 NIT VICTORY remains a proud moment in BYU athletic history, highlighting the team's talent and resilience during a competitive era in college basketball.

1966 NIT (National Invitation Tournament) Basketball Championship

In 1966, the BYU men's basketball team once again made history by winning the National Invitation Tournament (NIT) championship, marking their second NIT title. This victory solidified BYU's reputation as a strong competitor in college basketball during that era.

Key Details of the Championship:

- Tournament Journey: BYU had a remarkable run in the tournament, demonstrating skill and teamwork as they faced various opponents. Their success was highlighted by a series of impressive performances throughout the tournament.

- Final Game: The championship game took place at Madison Square Garden in New York City, where BYU faced Kentucky. The Cougars won a thrilling contest, finishing with a score of 93-89. The game was notable for its intensity and high level of play.

- Star Players:

  o Kurt Bennion was a standout performer for BYU, providing crucial scoring and leadership throughout the tournament.

  o Morris "Mo" Smith also played a significant role, contributing key points and rebounds that helped secure the championship.

Historical Significance:

- Back-to-Back Titles: The 1966 victory, following their previous NIT championship in 1951, showcased BYU's consistent excellence in basketball and contributed to the program's legacy.

- National Recognition: Winning the NIT in 1966 further established BYU as a competitive force in college basketball, attracting attention from fans and recruits alike. It also highlighted the growing prominence of the program under head coach Stan Watts.

THE 1966 NIT CHAMPIONSHIP remains a significant achievement in BYU's athletic history, reflecting the team's talent and dedication during a pivotal period for the program.

1970 Track and Field co- National Champions

In 1970, the BYU men's track and field team achieved a remarkable feat by scoring 35 points to claim a share of the national title at the NCAA Outdoor Track and Field Championships held from June 16-18 at Drake University in Des Moines, Iowa. They shared the title with Kansas and Oregon. This victory marked a significant milestone in BYU athletics, highlighting the program's strength and competitiveness on the national stage.

Key Highlights of the 1970 NCAA Outdoor Track and Field Championships:

1. OUTSTANDING TEAM Performance:

o The BYU team showcased exceptional talent and depth across multiple events, contributing to their total of 35 points, which was enough to tie for the national championship. This performance demonstrated the Cougars' ability to compete with the best teams in the country.

2. Notable Athletes:

o Several standout athletes contributed significantly to BYU's success during the championships. Among them was Bob Redd, who earned accolades in various events, helping to secure crucial points for the team. Redd's performances were instrumental in the overall team score.

3. Strong Relay Teams:

○ BYU's relay teams also played a critical role in accumulating points throughout the competition. The strength of the relay squads underscored the team's depth and cohesion, as they competed fiercely against other top programs.

4. Historical Context:

○ This championship marked a significant moment in BYU's track and field history, establishing the program as a national contender. It was part of a broader trend of excellence in BYU athletics during this era.

5. Tough Competition:

○ The championships featured fierce competition from other powerhouse programs, making BYU's performance even more impressive. The ability to perform under pressure at a national event showcased the team's resilience and determination.

6. Coaching Influence:

○ The success of the team was supported by the coaching staff, who played a crucial role in developing the athletes and strategizing for the competition. Their guidance was key to preparing the team for the challenges of the national championship.

7. Legacy of the 1970 Championship:

○ The shared national title in 1970 laid the groundwork for future success in BYU track and field, inspiring subsequent generations of athletes and coaches. The achievement continues to be a point of pride for the program.

8. Recognition and Impact:

○ BYU's success at the 1970 NCAA Outdoor Track and Field Championships garnered recognition within the collegiate athletics community. The championship win enhanced BYU's reputation and contributed to the growth of the track and field program.

Conclusion:

BYU'S ACHIEVEMENT IN scoring 35 points to share the national title at the 1970 NCAA Outdoor Track and Field Championships was a landmark moment in the program's history. The combination of outstanding individual performances, strong relay teams, and effective coaching culminated in this significant victory. This championship remains a proud highlight in BYU athletics and continues to inspire current and future student-athletes.

1980 The Miracle Bowl vs SMU

The 1980 Miracle Bowl stands as one of the most dramatic and memorable moments in college football history. In a thrilling come-from-behind victory, the BYU Cougars erased a 20-point deficit in the final minutes of the Holiday Bowl to defeat Southern Methodist University (SMU) 46-45. The game's defining moment was a last-second Hail Mary pass from quarterback Jim McMahon, cementing the game as a legendary chapter in both BYU football and college football lore.

The 1980 BYU team, coached by LaVell Edwards, came into the Holiday Bowl with a 11-1 record and one of the nation's top offenses, largely due to Edwards' innovative passing schemes. On the other side, SMU boasted an explosive offense of its own, powered by their famed "Pony Express" backfield duo of Eric Dickerson and Craig James. SMU, with its potent running game, controlled the majority of the matchup, and for much of the contest, BYU struggled to keep pace.

The first half was dominated by SMU, who took advantage of BYU's defensive struggles and capitalized on their powerful ground attack. By the fourth quarter, SMU held a commanding 45-25 lead with less than four minutes remaining. With the game seemingly out of reach, most fans and analysts thought SMU had the victory well in hand. However, BYU's players and their fearless quarterback Jim McMahon had other ideas.

McMahon, who had already established himself as one of the best passers in college football, engineered a miraculous comeback in those final minutes. First, McMahon led the Cougars on a quick scoring drive to cut the deficit to 45-31. After a successful onside kick recovery,

BYU scored again, narrowing the gap to 45-39 with less than two minutes left. With their second onside kick attempt failing and SMU regaining possession, BYU's hopes appeared to dwindle once more. But incredibly, BYU's defense managed to stop SMU, forcing a punt and giving McMahon one last opportunity to complete the comeback.

With time running out and BYU still down by six points, McMahon took the field for one final, desperate drive. As the seconds ticked away, BYU moved the ball downfield but still needed a miracle. With just three seconds left on the clock and the ball at SMU's 41-yard line, McMahon launched a high, arching Hail Mary pass into the end zone. Surrounded by defenders, BYU tight end Clay Brown leaped into the air and, in a moment of pure magic, came down with the ball for a game-tying touchdown.

The stadium erupted in disbelief, but the drama wasn't over yet. BYU still needed to convert the extra point to secure the victory. Kicker Kurt Gunther stepped up and calmly delivered the winning point, completing BYU's improbable 46-45 win.

The Miracle Bowl was not only a testament to Jim McMahon's resilience and leadership but also to the never-say-die attitude that LaVell Edwards instilled in his players. BYU's ability to remain focused and determined, even in the face of a 20-point deficit with only minutes remaining, became a defining characteristic of the team's success under Edwards.

McMahon's performance in the Miracle Bowl became the stuff of legend. He finished the game with 446 passing yards and four touchdowns, solidifying his place as one of the greatest quarterbacks in BYU history. For SMU, the loss was a heartbreaker, as their powerful offense and seemingly insurmountable lead evaporated in a matter of minutes. The game also added to the mystique of LaVell Edwards' innovative offensive strategies, which relied heavily on the passing game, a novel approach at the time.

The 1980 Holiday Bowl remains one of the most iconic games in college football history, and the term "Miracle Bowl" is still used to describe the unlikely and incredible events of that night. For BYU, the victory was a major stepping stone in the program's rise to national prominence, a journey that would culminate in their 1984 national championship. For fans and players alike, the Miracle Bowl is remembered as a defining moment of hope, perseverance, and the belief that anything is possible in sports.

To this day, the image of Jim McMahon's Hail Mary pass and Clay Brown's leaping catch lives on in the hearts of BYU fans, encapsulating the spirit of what became known as the "Miracle Bowl."

1980 Jim McMahon sets passing record

In 1979, Jim McMahon did not set the NCAA record for most passing yards in a season. However, he began to make a name for himself as a talented quarterback at BYU during that time, playing as a backup to starter Marc Wilson. McMahon's breakthrough year came in 1980 when he became the starting quarterback and helped establish BYU's reputation as a pass-heavy offense.

1980 Jim McMahon Breakthrough:

- Passing Record: In 1980, McMahon set the NCAA single-season passing yards record with 4,571 yards, breaking the previous record and helping to cement BYU's identity as a high-powered passing team under head coach LaVell Edwards.

- Touchdowns: He also threw 47 touchdown passes that season, leading BYU to a 12-1 record and victory in the 1980 Holiday Bowl, where McMahon's legendary Hail Mary pass to win the game put both him and BYU football on the map.

MCMAHON'S DOMINANCE continued into the 1981 season, where he finished third in the Heisman Trophy voting and set more NCAA records. His success was key to BYU becoming known as the "Quarterback Factory" in college football.

BYU football's best season is widely considered to be 1984, when the Cougars won the national championship, marking the pinnacle of the program's history.

Key Highlights of the 1984 BYU Football Season:

1. Perfect Record: BYU finished the season with a perfect 13-0 record, becoming the only undefeated team in Division I-A football that year.

2. Quarterback Play: The team was led by senior quarterback Robbie Bosco, who threw for 3,875 yards and 33 touchdowns despite battling injuries during the season.

3. Signature Wins: BYU opened the season with a victory over defending national champion Pittsburgh and secured several dominant wins throughout the year.

4. Holiday Bowl Victory: The Cougars capped their season with a 24-17 win over Michigan in the Holiday Bowl, a game in which Bosco played through injuries to lead BYU to victory. This win helped BYU secure the No. 1 ranking in both the AP and Coaches polls.

5. National Championship: After the season, BYU was crowned the national champion, becoming the first and only team from a non-power conference to win a national title in the modern era of college football.

Other Great Seasons:

- 1996: BYU finished 14-1, won the Cotton Bowl, and was ranked No. 5 in the final AP poll, one of the best finishes in program history.

- 2001: The Cougars started the season 12-0, led by quarterback Brandon Doman and running back Luke Staley, who won the Doak Walker Award as the nation's top running back.

WHILE BYU HAS HAD MANY strong seasons, the 1984 national championship season stands out as the greatest in the program's history.

1981 Women's Volleyball Final Four

The 1981 Women's Volleyball Final Four marked a pivotal moment for Brigham Young University's (BYU) women's volleyball team as they made their first NCAA Final Four appearance. This achievement highlighted the growth and development of the program, which had been steadily gaining momentum under the leadership of coach Elaine Michaelis.

During the 1981 season, the team exhibited exceptional skill and teamwork, advancing through the regional rounds to secure a place in the NCAA tournament. Their Final Four appearance was significant not only for the program but also for BYU athletics, as it showcased the talent and dedication of the women's volleyball team on a national stage. This milestone laid the foundation for future successes and helped raise the profile of BYU's women's volleyball program in collegiate athletics.

In BYU's 1981 women's volleyball team's historic journey to the NCAA Final Four, several standout players contributed to their success. Some key figures include:

1. Tanya Jones – A dominant force in the middle, Jones was known for her powerful presence at the net, both in blocking and attacking. Her height and athleticism made her a crucial asset for BYU during the 1981 season.
2. Linda Evans – As one of the top setters on the team, Evans played a pivotal role in directing BYU's offense. Her leadership and precision in setting allowed the team's attackers to thrive.
3. Sue Stokes – Stokes was a reliable and consistent performer

for BYU, known for her defensive skills and ability to contribute to the team's all-around play.

Under the coaching of Elaine Michaelis, who was a driving force in the development of the program, these players helped push BYU to its first-ever Final Four appearance. Michaelis herself would become one of the most respected figures in women's collegiate volleyball history. These athletes and their coach helped solidify BYU's standing as a competitive force in NCAA women's volleyball, paving the way for future success.

1981 NCAA National Golf Championship

In 1981, Brigham Young University's (BYU) men's golf team, under the leadership of coach Karl Tucker, won its first and only NCAA National Championship. The victory marked a historic moment for the program, as it solidified BYU's presence in collegiate golf. Tucker, who had coached at BYU for many years, led a talented team that outperformed other top schools in the competition. The championship remains a proud achievement in the university's athletic history and is often regarded as a testament to the strength of BYU's golf program during that era.

BYU's 1981 men's golf team featured several standout players who contributed to the school's NCAA National Championship victory. The top players included:

1. Rick Fehr – One of the most talented members of the team, Fehr went on to have a successful professional career on the PGA Tour. He was an All-American and one of the key contributors to BYU's championship run.
2. Bobby Clampett – Although Clampett turned professional before the 1981 championship, he was instrumental in the team's rise to prominence during his collegiate career at BYU. He was an All-American and one of the best amateurs of the time.
3. Keith Clearwater – Clearwater was another essential player on the 1981 squad. Like Fehr, he later had a solid professional career, including two PGA Tour wins.
4. Dick Zokol – A Canadian golfer, Zokol was a steady

presence on the team and later found success on the PGA Tour and Canadian golf scene.

These players, under the guidance of coach Karl Tucker, helped BYU claim its first and only NCAA golf championship, making it a legendary moment in the program's history.

1981 Danny Ainge in Sweet 16 win over Notre Dame

In the 1981 NCAA basketball tournament, BYU's Danny Ainge delivered one of the most memorable moments in the program's history with his coast-to-coast drive in the final seconds of the Sweet 16 game against Notre Dame. With the game tied and time winding down, Ainge grabbed a rebound, dribbled the length of the court, and scored a crucial basket, lifting BYU to a 51-50 victory. This dramatic play sent BYU to the Elite Eight for the first time in school history.

Ainge's performance was a defining moment of his college career and remains a celebrated highlight in BYU basketball history. His leadership and clutch play exemplified his exceptional skills and played a key role in BYU's impressive run in the tournament.

In the 1981 NCAA basketball tournament, BYU's run to the Elite Eight came to an end with a loss to Virginia. In the Elite Eight matchup, Virginia defeated BYU with a final score of 72-49. Despite the setback, BYU's performance in the tournament, highlighted by Danny Ainge's dramatic coast-to-coast drive in the Sweet 16, was a significant achievement for the program and remains a notable part of its history.

Danny Ainge is one of BYU's most celebrated athletes and a significant figure in basketball history. Here's a closer look at his career and achievements:

College Career at BYU (1977-1981)

- Position: Guard

● Notable Achievements:

○ 1981 Sweet 16: Ainge's famous coast-to-coast drive in the final seconds against Notre Dame remains one of the most iconic moments in BYU basketball history.

○ 1981 Elite Eight: Although BYU lost to Virginia in the Elite Eight, Ainge's performance throughout the tournament was a key factor in the team's success.

○ Awards: Ainge was named an All-American and was a key player for BYU, leading the team with impressive statistics and leadership.

Professional Career

● NBA Career:

○ Drafted: Ainge was selected by the Portland Trail Blazers as the 31st overall pick in the 1981 NBA Draft.

○ Teams: He played for several teams, including the Portland Trail Blazers, Boston Celtics, Sacramento Kings, and Phoenix Suns.

○ Achievements: Ainge won two NBA championships with the Boston Celtics (1984, 1986) and was known for his versatile play and clutch performances.

● NBA Executive:

○ Boston Celtics: After retiring as a player, Ainge transitioned into an executive role with the Celtics. He served as the General Manager and later as the President of Basketball Operations. Under his leadership, the Celtics won the 2008 NBA Championship.

Legacy

● Hall of Fame: Danny Ainge was inducted into the BYU Athletic Hall of Fame and is recognized as one of the greatest players in BYU history.

● Versatility: Known for his ability to play both guard positions and his knack for clutch shooting, Ainge's impact on the game was felt both on and off the court.

DANNY AINGE'S CONTRIBUTIONS to basketball, both at the collegiate and professional levels, have cemented his legacy as one of the sport's prominent figures. His leadership, skills, and impact on the game have made him a respected and influential name in basketball history.

1983 LaVell Edwards 100th Victory

In 1983, LaVell Edwards reached a significant milestone in his coaching career by earning his 100th victory as the head coach of the BYU Cougars football team. This achievement not only marked a personal milestone for Edwards but also further solidified his legacy as one of the most successful and influential coaches in college football history.

Key Highlights of LaVell Edwards' 100th Victory:

1. HISTORIC CAREER:

○ LaVell Edwards became the first head coach in BYU football history to achieve 100 wins, underscoring his impact on the program. His coaching tenure began in 1972 and spanned over three decades, during which he transformed BYU into a national powerhouse.

2. Memorable Game:

○ Edwards achieved this milestone victory on October 1, 1983, in a game against New Mexico, where BYU won decisively with a score of 48-7. The win not only celebrated Edwards' achievement but also demonstrated the Cougars' dominance that season.

3. Offensive Innovations:

○ Under Edwards' leadership, BYU became known for its innovative and high-powered offense, often referred to as the "Air Attack." This offensive strategy contributed to the development of many successful quarterbacks, including Jim McMahon, who would go on to achieve great success in the NFL.

4. Impact on College Football:

○ Edwards' coaching style and emphasis on the passing game had a lasting influence on college football, leading to a shift in how teams approached offensive strategies. His success helped put BYU on the national map and paved the way for the program to compete against some of the best teams in the country.

5. National Recognition:

○ The 1983 season was significant for BYU as the team finished with a strong record and was consistently ranked among the top teams in the nation. Edwards' achievement of 100 victories further elevated the program's stature and attracted more attention from recruits and fans alike.

6. Legacy:

○ LaVell Edwards is remembered not only for his wins but also for his character and leadership. He instilled values of integrity, sportsmanship, and dedication in his players, making a lasting impact on their lives both on and off the field.

Conclusion:

LAVELL EDWARDS' 100TH career victory in 1983 was a monumental moment for him and the BYU football program. This milestone not only highlighted his coaching prowess but also signified the growth and success of BYU football under his leadership. Edwards' legacy continues to resonate within the program and college football, making him a legendary figure in the sport.

1983 Western Athletic basketball championship

In 1983, Fred Roberts led BYU's men's basketball team to the Western Athletic Conference (WAC) title, marking one of the strongest seasons in the program's history. Roberts, a standout forward, was instrumental in BYU's success that season, showcasing his versatility, scoring ability, and leadership on the court.

Key highlights from the 1982-1983 season:

- WAC Championship: With Roberts as their star player, BYU won the WAC basketball title, securing their place as the top team in the conference. Roberts' ability to score, rebound, and defend made him a pivotal figure in BYU's run to the championship.

- NCAA Tournament: BYU's success in the WAC earned them a berth in the NCAA Tournament. The Cougars made it to the second round, further solidifying their reputation as a top-tier team that season.

Fred Roberts' leadership and talent during the 1983 season helped elevate BYU basketball to new heights, making it one of the program's most memorable years. After his collegiate career, Roberts went on to have a solid NBA career, further proving his basketball pedigree.

In 1983, Fred Roberts led BYU's men's basketball team to the Western Athletic Conference (WAC) title, marking one of the strongest seasons in the program's history. Roberts, a standout forward, was instrumental in BYU's success that season, showcasing his versatility, scoring ability, and leadership on the court.

Key highlights from the 1982-1983 season:

- **WAC Championship:** With Roberts as their star player, BYU won the WAC basketball title, securing their place as the top team in the conference. Roberts' ability to score, rebound, and defend made him a pivotal figure in BYU's run to the championship.

- **NCAA Tournament:** BYU's success in the WAC earned them a berth in the NCAA Tournament. The Cougars made it to the second round, further solidifying their reputation as a top-tier team that season.

Fred Roberts' leadership and talent during the 1983 season helped elevate BYU basketball to new heights, making it one of the program's most memorable years. After his collegiate career, Roberts went on to have a solid NBA career, further proving his basketball pedigree.

1983 Steve Young's performance in the Holiday Bowl

Steve Young's performance in the 1983 Holiday Bowl is one of the most memorable in BYU football history, but the outcome was different than described. In that game, BYU lost 21-17 to Missouri in a thrilling contest.

Young had an impressive individual performance, throwing for 328 yards and one touchdown while also rushing for 100 yards. However, BYU was unable to secure the win, as Missouri held on for the victory. Despite the loss, Young's efforts in the Holiday Bowl, along with his stellar 1983 season, helped solidify his legacy at BYU. He was later named a consensus All-American and finished second in the Heisman Trophy voting that year.

BYU has a rich tradition of producing outstanding quarterbacks, many of whom have gone on to have successful careers in both college football and the NFL. Some of the best BYU quarterbacks include:

1. Ty Detmer (1987–1991)

- Accolades: He won the Heisman Trophy in 1990, the first and only BYU player to do so. Detmer was a two-time All-American and set numerous NCAA passing records during his career.

- Career Stats: Detmer threw for over 15,000 yards and 121 touchdowns during his time at BYU, making him one of the most prolific passers in college football history.

• NFL Career: He played in the NFL for several teams over a 14-year career.

2. Steve Young (1981–1983)

• Accolades: A consensus All-American in 1983 and runner-up for the Heisman Trophy, Young is one of the most dynamic dual-threat quarterbacks in BYU history. He threw for 3,902 yards and 33 touchdowns in his senior year, while also rushing for 444 yards and 8 touchdowns.

• NFL Career: Young went on to have a legendary NFL career, winning three Super Bowls (two as a backup and one as a starter) and two NFL MVPs with the San Francisco 49ers. He was inducted into the Pro Football Hall of Fame in 2005.

3. Jim McMahon (1977–1981)

• Accolades: McMahon was a two-time All-American and finished third in the Heisman voting in 1981. He led BYU to its first-ever Holiday Bowl victory in 1980 with a legendary comeback win over SMU, capped by his famous Hail Mary touchdown pass.

• Career Stats: He set several NCAA records for passing yards and touchdowns, and threw for 4,571 yards and 47 touchdowns in his senior season.

• NFL Career: McMahon went on to win a Super Bowl as the starting quarterback for the Chicago Bears in 1985 and had a successful NFL career spanning 15 years.

4. Zach Wilson (2018–2020)

● Accolades: Wilson had a breakout season in 2020, leading BYU to an 11-1 record. He finished his junior year with 3,692 passing yards, 33 touchdowns, and just 3 interceptions, making him a Heisman Trophy candidate.

● NFL Career: Wilson was drafted second overall in the 2021 NFL Draft by the New York Jets, making him one of the highest-drafted BYU players ever.

5. John Beck (2003–2006)

● Accolades: Beck was named Mountain West Conference Offensive Player of the Year in 2006 and led BYU to a 10-2 record and a win in the Las Vegas Bowl. His famous game-winning pass in the final seconds against Utah in 2006 is one of the most memorable plays in BYU history.

● Career Stats: He threw for 11,021 yards and 79 touchdowns during his college career.

6. Max Hall (2007–2009)

● Accolades: Hall was a three-year starter and is BYU's all-time leader in career wins as a quarterback, with a 32-7 record. He led BYU to three consecutive bowl games and a memorable upset win over No. 3 Oklahoma in 2009.

● Career Stats: He finished his career with 11,365 passing yards and 94 touchdowns.

7. Marc Wilson (1977–1979)

- Accolades: Wilson was a consensus All-American in 1979 and finished third in the Heisman Trophy voting that year. He set several NCAA passing records and was a key figure in establishing BYU's reputation as a passing powerhouse.

- NFL Career: Wilson was a first-round NFL draft pick and played 10 seasons in the NFL, winning two Super Bowls with the Oakland Raiders.

THESE QUARTERBACKS helped shape BYU's legacy as a "Quarterback Factory," known for producing prolific passers and leaders on the field. Many of them went on to have notable careers at the professional level.

1983 BYU football wins WAC

The 1983 BYU football team achieved a significant milestone by winning the Western Athletic Conference (WAC) Championship, finishing the season with an impressive record of 11-1. This season marked a key moment in the rise of BYU football, solidifying its reputation as a competitive force in college football.

Key Highlights of the 1983 Season:

1. WAC CHAMPIONSHIP:

○ BYU clinched the WAC title, showcasing their dominance in the conference. This championship was pivotal for the program, establishing BYU as a leading team in college football during the early 1980s.

2. Strong Season Record:

○ The Cougars finished the season with an 11-1 record, demonstrating their consistency and ability to perform at a high level throughout the season. The only loss came against the University of California, Berkeley.

3. Star Players:

○ Quarterback Jim McMahon played a crucial role in the team's success, leading the offense with his strong passing ability and leadership. He was known for his playmaking skills, which helped propel the Cougars to victory in several key games.

○ Other notable players included running back Mike S. Wilcox and wide receiver Clayton W. Ricks, who contributed significantly to the team's offensive performance.

4. Signature Wins:

○ The Cougars secured important victories during the season, including a notable win against Texas in the Holiday Bowl. This victory further cemented their status as a formidable opponent in college football.

5. Holiday Bowl Appearance:

○ After winning the WAC Championship, BYU earned a spot in the 1984 Holiday Bowl, where they faced the University of Michigan. The Cougars went on to win the game, capping off their successful season with a bowl victory.

6. Impact on the Program:

○ The success of the 1983 season set the stage for BYU's future achievements, contributing to the overall growth of the football program. It helped lay the groundwork for future successes, including the national championship run in 1984.

7. National Recognition:

○ The 1983 WAC Championship and strong season performance garnered national attention for BYU football. The team's success contributed to the growing popularity of college football in Utah and increased recruitment efforts for talented players.

8. Legacy of BYU Football:

○ The achievements of the 1983 team are remembered as part of BYU's rich football history. The foundation laid during this season helped establish the Cougars as a perennial contender in college football.

Conclusion:

BYU'S 1983 WAC CHAMPIONSHIP season was a pivotal moment in the program's history, marked by a strong record, key victories, and the emergence of standout players. This successful season not only solidified BYU's place in the WAC but also set the stage for future successes in the years to come, including the 1984 national championship. The legacy of the 1983 team continues to inspire current players and fans of BYU football.

1984 BYU wins the national football championship

The 1984 football season was a monumental year for Brigham Young University (BYU), as the Cougars capped off a perfect 13-0 record by winning the national championship. This achievement, which remains BYU's only national title in football, culminated with a hard-fought 24-17 victory over the University of Michigan in the Holiday Bowl. It was a season that not only showcased the team's talent but also catapulted the program into national prominence under the leadership of legendary head coach LaVell Edwards.

BYU entered the 1984 season coming off several successful years under Edwards, a coach known for his innovative passing offense. The Cougars were ranked No. 13 in the preseason polls, but few expected them to challenge for the national championship. However, led by senior quarterback Robbie Bosco and a talented group of players, the team quickly established itself as a force to be reckoned with.

The Cougars opened the season with a thrilling 20-14 victory over the No. 3-ranked Pittsburgh Panthers, immediately raising their profile on the national stage. From there, BYU rolled through its schedule, defeating opponents with a combination of offensive firepower and defensive grit. Their high-powered passing attack, orchestrated by Bosco, kept opposing defenses on their heels, and their ability to execute in critical moments set them apart.

As the regular season progressed, BYU continued to climb the national rankings. By the time they had completed their perfect 12-0 regular season, they found themselves in the conversation for the national championship. However, because BYU was a member of the Western

Athletic Conference (WAC), which was not considered a major football conference at the time, there were skeptics who doubted whether BYU deserved to be in the running for a national title. Despite these doubts, BYU was invited to play in the Holiday Bowl against Michigan, a respected Big Ten team that would provide the Cougars with a significant challenge.

The 1984 Holiday Bowl, played on December 21, 1984, in San Diego, California, was the stage for BYU's quest to solidify its championship claim. Michigan, although unranked at the time, was still a formidable opponent, and the game was expected to be a tough battle. Early on, it appeared as though BYU might be in trouble. Quarterback Robbie Bosco suffered a leg injury in the first quarter, which limited his mobility for the rest of the game. Despite the injury, Bosco remained in the game and continued to lead the offense.

Michigan took a 17-10 lead into the fourth quarter, but Bosco and the Cougars were not finished. In a gutsy performance, Bosco threw for 343 yards and two touchdowns, including the game-winning score in the final minutes. A critical interception by BYU's defense sealed the victory, and the Cougars emerged with a 24-17 win. The victory capped off BYU's perfect season and left them as the only undefeated team in college football that year.

In the final rankings, BYU was named the national champion by both the Associated Press (AP) and the Coaches' Poll, solidifying their place in history. Their championship was a watershed moment for both the program and for smaller schools outside the traditional power conferences. BYU's success in 1984 demonstrated that a team from a non-major conference could rise to the top of college football, provided they had the talent, determination, and coaching to do so.

For BYU, the 1984 season remains the pinnacle of its football history. It was a season marked by outstanding performances, particularly from

Robbie Bosco, and the leadership of LaVell Edwards, whose vision and coaching philosophy transformed the program into a national power. The Cougars' national championship win stands as a testament to the power of perseverance and belief in the face of adversity, and it remains one of the most memorable moments in college football history.

1984 Steve Young won Davey O'Brien Award

In 1984, Steve Young won the prestigious Davey O'Brien Award, recognizing him as the nation's top quarterback. This honor solidified Young's legacy as one of the greatest college quarterbacks of his time and a key figure in the history of BYU football.

During the 1983 season, Young had an outstanding performance for the BYU Cougars, throwing for over 3,900 yards and 33 touchdowns, while completing an astonishing 71.3% of his passes. His dual-threat ability, with both precise passing and impressive running skills, made him a dynamic and versatile quarterback. He rushed for 8 touchdowns as well, further showcasing his athleticism.

Young's performance led BYU to an 11-1 season, and he finished second in the Heisman Trophy voting that year. His winning of the Davey O'Brien Award marked him as the best quarterback in college football and laid the groundwork for his successful NFL career, where he would go on to become a Super Bowl champion and Hall of Fame quarterback.

The award was a major milestone in BYU football's rich quarterback tradition, further highlighting the program's ability to produce elite-level talent under the guidance of head coach LaVell Edwards.

1985 BYU women's cross country first NCAA national championship

In 1985, the BYU women's cross country team captured its first-ever NCAA national championship, marking a historic moment for the program and for women's collegiate cross country. Under the leadership of legendary head coach Patrick Shane, BYU emerged as a powerhouse, beginning a dynasty that would see them win four national titles over the next two decades.

Key Details of the 1985 Championship:

- Team Performance: BYU's runners delivered an outstanding team performance at the NCAA national meet, held in Milwaukee, Wisconsin. The Cougars' strategy of depth and strong pack running allowed them to accumulate a low score, which secured their place at the top of the podium.

- Top Runners:

○ Julie Jenkins was one of the team's standout performers, placing among the top finishers and leading the Cougars in the race.

○ Mary Schiess and Margo Carter also played key roles in BYU's scoring, with consistent performances that added to the team's overall dominance.

○ Jennifer Noble contributed to the team's overall strength, rounding out the runners who secured the victory.

Team Strategy and Depth:

PATRICK SHANE, A MASTER of coaching cross country, emphasized a strategy of team depth and pack running. BYU's runners were known for staying close together in races, minimizing the gaps between their top five scorers. This approach allowed them to consistently outperform teams with individual stars by scoring well across the board.

Historical Impact:

THE 1985 VICTORY WAS the first of BYU's four national championships under Coach Patrick Shane, who would go on to lead the team to additional titles in 1997, 1999, and 2001. This first win set the foundation for BYU women's cross country to become one of the most dominant programs in NCAA history. Shane's leadership, combined with the talent and dedication of his athletes, propelled BYU to long-term success on the national stage.

This championship also highlighted the growing strength of BYU women's athletics, showcasing the university's commitment to excellence in women's sports during an era of significant growth for collegiate women's programs.

1985 BYU football ranked No. 3

In 1985, quarterback Robbie Bosco had a standout season, leading the BYU Cougars to a remarkable 11-3 record and achieving a No. 3 national ranking in the final AP Poll. This season was pivotal in establishing Bosco's legacy as one of BYU's all-time great quarterbacks.

Key Highlights of the 1985 Season:

1. Record-Breaking Performance:

○ Bosco threw for over 4,000 yards, becoming one of the few quarterbacks at the time to reach this milestone in a single season. His ability to connect with receivers and make big plays downfield was instrumental in BYU's success.

2. Offensive Firepower:

○ The 1985 team featured a potent offense that utilized the passing game effectively, often referred to as the "Air Attack." Bosco's passing prowess, combined with the talent of his receiving corps, made BYU one of the most exciting teams to watch.

3. Signature Games:

○ The Cougars had several memorable games that season, including a significant victory over Miami, which was ranked No. 8 at the time. This win helped solidify BYU's reputation as a national contender and contributed to their high ranking.

4. WAC Championship:

○ BYU also claimed the Western Athletic Conference (WAC) title that year, further showcasing their dominance in the conference and setting the stage for a successful bowl game.

5. Cotton Bowl Appearance:

○ The Cougars' successful season culminated in a trip to the Cotton Bowl, where they faced the University of Oklahoma. Although BYU lost the game, the season as a whole was considered a tremendous success and elevated the program's national profile.

6. Robbie Bosco's Legacy:

○ Bosco's performance during the 1985 season helped him earn several accolades, including All-American honors and recognition as one of the top quarterbacks in college football. His leadership and playmaking ability contributed to the foundation of BYU's offensive success in the years to come.

Conclusion:

THE 1985 SEASON WAS a defining moment for BYU football, with Robbie Bosco at the helm. His impressive statistics and ability to lead the team to a top national ranking not only highlighted his talent but also reinforced BYU's status as a competitive force in college football during the 1980s.

1985 Steve Young finds his way to the NFL

Actually, Steve Young was not selected in the 1985 NFL Draft. After a stellar college career at BYU, Young had already signed with the Los Angeles Express of the USFL in 1984, bypassing the NFL Draft entirely. However, after the USFL folded, Young entered the NFL in 1985 when the Tampa Bay Buccaneers obtained his rights by signing him to a contract. He struggled with the Buccaneers and was eventually traded to the San Francisco 49ers in 1987, where he became a Hall of Fame quarterback.

Steve Young's NFL peak came during the early to mid-1990s, particularly from 1992 to 1994, when he was at the height of his abilities and success. Some key highlights of his peak include:

1. 1992 NFL MVP Season

- MVP Award: Young won his first NFL MVP award in 1992.

- Statistics: He led the league in passer rating (107.0) and threw for 25 touchdowns with only 7 interceptions. His 68% completion rate and 3,465 passing yards solidified his status as the NFL's top quarterback.

- Dual-threat ability: Young rushed for 537 yards and 4 touchdowns that season, displaying his renowned scrambling ability.

2. 1994 Super Bowl Season

- Super Bowl XXIX Champion: Young led the San Francisco 49ers to a victory in Super Bowl XXIX, defeating the San Diego Chargers 49–26.

- Super Bowl MVP: He was named the Super Bowl MVP after a legendary performance where he threw a Super Bowl record 6 touchdown passes, which still stands.

- Second MVP Award: He also won his second league MVP award in 1994.

- Stats dominance: That season, he led the NFL in passer rating (112.8), completion percentage (70.3%), and threw for 3,969 yards with 35 touchdowns and 10 interceptions. He also added 289 rushing yards and 7 touchdowns on the ground.

3. Sustained Excellence (1991–1998)

- During this period, Young consistently led the NFL in passer rating (six times) and was a perennial Pro Bowl and All-Pro selection.

- He led the league in completion percentage five times and touchdown passes four times.

- He became the first player to record a passer rating of over 100 in four consecutive seasons (1991–1994).

Legacy of Young's Peak

YOUNG'S PEAK SOLIDIFIED his reputation as one of the most efficient quarterbacks in NFL history, known for his pinpoint accuracy, elite mobility, and football intelligence. His ability to succeed both as a passer and a runner set him apart from many other quarterbacks of his era.

1990 Ty Detmer Stuns Number 1 Miami

In 1990, BYU achieved a stunning victory by defeating the No. 1-ranked Miami Hurricanes 28-21, a win that was one of the biggest upsets of the college football season. This game was particularly significant for BYU and its quarterback, Ty Detmer, who played a pivotal role in the upset.

Key Highlights of the Game:

- Date: September 8, 1990

- Location: Miami, Florida

- Result: BYU 28, Miami 21

Ty Detmer's Performance:

- Quarterback: Ty Detmer delivered an outstanding performance, throwing for 299 yards and four touchdowns. His play was crucial in BYU's ability to overcome the defending national champions.

- Heisman Campaign: Detmer's performance in this game was a significant boost to his Heisman Trophy campaign. His impressive play throughout the season and in this game helped him eventually win the Heisman Trophy that year.

Impact of the Victory:

- National Attention: The win was a major headline and put BYU on the national stage, showcasing their ability to compete against top-tier programs.

- Heisman Trophy: Detmer's performance throughout the season, including the game against Miami, earned him the 1990 Heisman Trophy, making him the second BYU player to win the prestigious award.

Legacy:

Historic Win: The victory over Miami remains one of the greatest achievements in BYU football history and is a defining moment for the program.

TY DETMER: DETMER'S success in 1990 solidified his place as one of the most prominent quarterbacks in college football history and remains a celebrated figure in BYU athletics.

This game is often remembered as a classic example of how a single game can have a profound impact on a player's career and a team's legacy.

1990 Ty Detmer wins Heisman Trophy

In 1990, BYU quarterback Ty Detmer etched his name in college football history by becoming the first Cougar to win the prestigious Heisman Trophy. Detmer's remarkable season not only solidified his place as one of the greatest quarterbacks in NCAA history but also brought national attention to Brigham Young University's football program, which was already known for producing top-tier talent under legendary head coach LaVell Edwards.

Ty Detmer's road to the Heisman began long before the 1990 season. Detmer had shown flashes of brilliance in previous seasons, but it was his junior year that elevated him to elite status. Playing in LaVell Edwards' pass-heavy offense, Detmer had the perfect stage to showcase his skills as a cerebral and highly accurate passer. Edwards' offensive system, which focused on spreading the field and utilizing the passing game to dissect defenses, was ideal for a quarterback with Detmer's intelligence, quick decision-making, and accuracy.

The 1990 season started with high expectations, as Detmer had already earned a reputation as one of the top quarterbacks in the country. From the first game of the season, it was clear that Detmer was on another level. In a thrilling season opener, BYU faced defending national champion Miami, which came into the game ranked No. 1 in the nation. Despite being the underdogs, BYU, led by Detmer, pulled off a shocking 28-21 upset. Detmer threw for 406 yards and three touchdowns, putting himself squarely in the Heisman conversation early in the season. That victory not only set the tone for BYU's season but also demonstrated that Detmer could perform against the very best.

Throughout the 1990 season, Detmer continued to rack up eye-popping statistics. He finished the year with an astounding 5,188 passing yards, breaking numerous NCAA records in the process. He also threw 41 touchdown passes and had a completion percentage of 64.2%, all while leading BYU to a 10-3 record. Detmer's ability to read defenses, make quick decisions, and deliver accurate throws in high-pressure situations made him nearly unstoppable, and his performances week after week kept him in the national spotlight.

By the time the Heisman Trophy ceremony arrived in December 1990, Detmer was considered the clear frontrunner. He had not only put up record-breaking numbers but had also led BYU to several high-profile victories, including the iconic win over Miami. When Detmer was announced as the winner of the Heisman Trophy, he became the first player in BYU history to receive the prestigious award, joining the ranks of college football's all-time greats. He beat out other top contenders, including Notre Dame's Raghib "Rocket" Ismail and Colorado's Eric Bieniemy, to claim the trophy.

Detmer's Heisman win was more than just a personal achievement; it was a moment of validation for BYU's football program. Under LaVell Edwards, BYU had become known for its explosive offenses and innovative passing schemes, but the Heisman victory helped elevate the program to new heights of national recognition. Detmer's success symbolized the rise of the pass-heavy offensive systems that BYU had pioneered, and it showed that even a relatively small program from outside the traditional power conferences could produce the best player in the nation.

After winning the Heisman, Detmer would go on to have a long and successful football career, both in college and in the NFL. He returned to BYU for his senior season, continuing to shatter records, and finished his collegiate career with more than 15,000 passing yards, the most in NCAA history at the time. Although he didn't achieve the same level of success in the NFL, Detmer's impact on college football, particularly at BYU, remains undeniable.

Ty Detmer's 1990 Heisman Trophy victory is a cornerstone in BYU football history, symbolizing the height of the program's national prominence. Detmer's accomplishments on the field, combined with his leadership and poise, made him a fitting recipient of college football's most prestigious award. His Heisman win continues to inspire generations of BYU players and fans, serving as a reminder of what is possible through hard work, determination, and talent.

2001 Men's National Volleyball Championship

In 2001, BYU's men's volleyball team won their second NCAA National Championship, showcasing their dominance in the sport. Here's a closer look at that championship:

2001 Men's Volleyball National Championship:

- Date: May 12, 2001

- Location: Pauley Pavilion, Los Angeles, California

- Opponent: UCLA Bruins

Match Highlights:

- Result: BYU defeated UCLA in straight sets with scores of 30-23, 30-25, and 30-22.

- Performance: BYU's victory was marked by a dominant performance, with strong play in both offense and defense throughout the match.

Key Players:

- Mike Wall: Wall was a standout player for BYU, known for his powerful hitting and all-around performance. He was instrumental in leading the team to victory.

- Ryan Millar: Millar, another key player, contributed significantly both at the net and in defense, helping BYU control the match.

Coaching Staff:

- Carl McGown: The head coach of BYU's men's volleyball team, McGown's leadership and strategic acumen were crucial in guiding the team to their second national title.

Impact and Legacy:

- Second National Title: This win marked BYU's second NCAA men's volleyball championship, adding to their first title won in 1999.

- Program Success: The 2001 championship solidified BYU's reputation as a powerhouse in collegiate men's volleyball and highlighted their ability to compete at the highest level.

THE 2001 NATIONAL CHAMPIONSHIP was a significant achievement for BYU's men's volleyball program, demonstrating their skill, teamwork, and ability to perform under pressure.

2001 BYU softball makes NCAA Tournament

In 2001, the BYU softball team made history by securing its first-ever appearance in the NCAA Tournament, marking a significant milestone for the program. This achievement represented a turning point that laid the foundation for future success in BYU softball.

Key Highlights of the 2001 Season:

1. HISTORIC ACHIEVEMENT:

○ BYU's qualification for the NCAA Tournament was a momentous occasion for the program, highlighting years of hard work, dedication, and growth. It was a significant step in establishing BYU softball as a competitive force in collegiate athletics.

2. Strong Regular Season:

○ The Cougars had a successful regular season, finishing with a solid record that demonstrated their improvement and potential. Their performance in conference play was particularly noteworthy, helping them secure an NCAA Tournament berth.

3. Key Players:

○ The team featured standout players who contributed significantly to their success during the season. Notable performances from these athletes played a crucial role in the Cougars' path to the tournament.

4. WAC Championship:

○ BYU's successful season was highlighted by a strong showing in the Western Athletic Conference (WAC) Championship, where they showcased their talent and resilience. Winning games in the conference tournament was instrumental in earning their NCAA bid.

5. NCAA Tournament Experience:

○ Competing in the NCAA Tournament provided the Cougars with invaluable experience against high-caliber teams. Although they faced tough competition, the opportunity to participate in such a prestigious event was an important learning experience for the players and coaching staff.

6. Impact on the Program:

○ The 2001 NCAA Tournament appearance helped elevate the profile of BYU softball and attract attention to the program. It inspired future generations of players and set a standard for excellence within the team.

7. Community and Fan Support:

○ The Cougars enjoyed strong support from fans and the local community, who rallied behind the team during their historic run. This support created an energized atmosphere around BYU softball and contributed to the program's momentum.

8. Legacy of Success:

○ The 2001 season laid the groundwork for continued success in subsequent years. BYU softball has since established itself as a competitive program, consistently making NCAA Tournament appearances and achieving significant milestones.

Conclusion:

BYU SOFTBALL'S FIRST NCAA Tournament appearance in 2001 was a groundbreaking moment for the program, symbolizing years of dedication and hard work. The experience of competing at the national level not only boosted the team's confidence but also laid the foundation for future success. This historic achievement continues to resonate within the BYU athletic community, inspiring current and future student-athletes.

2001 BYU running back Luke Staley wins Doak Walker Award

In 2001, BYU running back Luke Staley achieved a prestigious honor by winning the Doak Walker Award, which is awarded annually to the nation's top college football running back. This accolade marked a significant milestone in Staley's career and highlighted his exceptional talent on the field.

Key Highlights of Luke Staley's 2001 Season:

1. OUTSTANDING PERFORMANCE:

○ Luke Staley had a remarkable season, rushing for 1,400 yards and scoring 24 touchdowns, showcasing his explosive speed, agility, and ability to break tackles. His performance was pivotal in leading BYU to a successful season.

2. Record-Breaking Achievements:

○ Staley set several records during the 2001 season, including the highest number of rushing touchdowns in a season for BYU. His impressive statistics contributed to his recognition as one of the best running backs in college football.

3. Key Games:

○ Staley had standout performances in crucial games, including a memorable game against Hawaii, where he rushed for over 300 yards and scored multiple touchdowns, demonstrating his ability to perform under pressure.

4. Team Success:

○ His contributions helped BYU finish the season with a strong record, securing a bowl game appearance and showcasing the team's overall talent and depth.

5. Doak Walker Award Recognition:

○ Winning the Doak Walker Award was a crowning achievement for Staley, placing him among the elite running backs in college football history. The award is named after the legendary Texas A&M running back and recognizes excellence in performance, sportsmanship, and character.

6. Legacy at BYU:

○ Staley's success left a lasting legacy at BYU. He became a role model for future running backs in the program and was celebrated for his hard work and dedication both on and off the field.

7. Post-College Career:

○ After winning the Doak Walker Award, Staley was drafted into the NFL, although his professional career was hindered by injuries. Despite the challenges, his college accomplishments solidified his place in BYU sports history.

Conclusion:

LUKE STALEY'S VICTORY in the 2001 Doak Walker Award was a significant achievement for both him and the BYU football program. His extraordinary performance during the season not only earned him national recognition but also contributed to the rich legacy of BYU athletics. Staley's success continues to inspire future generations of athletes in the program.

2002 Women's Cross Country National Championship

In 2002, BYU's women's cross country team captured their third NCAA National Championship, solidifying their status as a powerhouse in the sport. The team, coached by Patrick Shane, dominated the competition and further established BYU's women's cross country program as one of the most successful in the nation.

Key highlights from the 2002 championship season:

- Team Performance: BYU's runners delivered an impressive team effort, placing multiple athletes in the top finishes of the race. The Cougars scored 85 points, comfortably outpacing their closest competitor, Stanford, who finished with 113 points.

- Top Runners: Leading the way for BYU were standouts like Michaela Manova, who finished 6th individually, and Kassi Andersen, who placed 10th. Their strong performances were instrumental in securing the victory.

- Dominance in the Sport: This win marked BYU's third NCAA title (after wins in 1997 and 1999), further establishing the program as a dominant force in women's cross country. Their consistency at the national level made them one of the most feared and respected teams in the sport during that era.

The 2002 victory capped off another stellar season for BYU women's cross country, adding to the legacy of Coach Patrick Shane and the program's enduring success in NCAA competition.

2006 BYU football wins their first Mountain West Conference (MWC) championship.

In 2006, the BYU Cougars football team achieved a significant milestone by winning their first Mountain West Conference (MWC) championship. This victory was particularly noteworthy as it marked the end of the University of Utah's dominance in the longstanding rivalry between the two schools.

Key Details of the Championship Season:

- Regular Season Record: BYU finished the regular season with an impressive 11-2 record, which included a crucial 20-7 victory over Utah in the final game of the season. This win not only secured the MWC title but also a sense of pride in the rivalry.

- Strong Performers:

  ○ John Beck: As the starting quarterback, Beck had a standout season, throwing for over 3,500 yards and 32 touchdowns. His leadership and passing ability were instrumental in the Cougars' success.

  ○ Manase Tonga: The running back played a key role in the offense, providing balance with his rushing ability.

  ○ Defense: The BYU defense, led by players like Brock Atkinson and Keenan L. Peppers, was also pivotal, consistently making plays to secure wins.

Championship Game:

BYU'S JOURNEY CULMINATED in the 2006 MWC Championship Game, where they faced off against Samford. The Cougars dominated the game, showcasing their strength and talent, and solidifying their status as conference champions.

Historical Significance:

- Rivalry Shift: This championship ended a four-year run of dominance by Utah in the rivalry and shifted the momentum back in favor of BYU. It reignited the competitive spirit in one of college football's most intense rivalries.

- Foundation for Future Success: Winning the MWC title set the stage for continued success in subsequent seasons, reinforcing BYU's reputation as a top program in college football.

THE 2006 MOUNTAIN WEST Conference championship remains a defining moment in BYU football history, highlighting a successful season and marking a new chapter in the rivalry with Utah.

2007 the BYU gymnastics team wins Mountain West Conference (MWC) championship,

In 2007, the BYU gymnastics team made history by winning its first-ever Mountain West Conference (MWC) championship, a monumental achievement for the program. The team, led by head coach Brad Cattermole, put together a season of exceptional performances, culminating in their victory at the conference championship meet.

Standout gymnasts during this season included:

- Lisa Willis – Known for her consistency and grace, Willis was a top performer on the balance beam and floor exercise, helping the team achieve high scores in key events.

- Madeleine Johnson – Johnson's power and precision on vault and uneven bars contributed significantly to the team's overall score.

- Hayley Jensen – An all-around competitor, Jensen excelled in multiple events, providing the team with valuable points across the board.

The win was a landmark moment for BYU gymnastics, marking the first time the team had captured a conference title. This success was not only a testament to the talent and dedication of the athletes but also a reflection of the strong coaching and support staff that helped guide them to victory. The 2007 championship set a new standard for the program, elevating BYU gymnastics to a new level of national recognition.

2009 National Champions Men's Intramural Soccer

In 2009, BYU's men's soccer team captured the NIRSA (National Intramural-Recreational Sports Association) National Championship, marking a significant milestone for the program. Although BYU's men's soccer team competed as a club program rather than an NCAA-sanctioned team, this victory was still a major achievement in collegiate club soccer.

Key points from the 2009 season:

- National Championship Victory: BYU's men's soccer team won the NIRSA national title by defeating Weber State 1-0 in the championship game. This win crowned them as the best collegiate club soccer team in the country.

- BYU's Dominance: The 2009 championship was a reflection of BYU's strength and consistency in the club soccer scene. The program had long been competitive in NIRSA play, and the national title cemented their reputation as a powerhouse.

- Historical Significance: Although BYU had previously competed in the Premier Development League (PDL), this NIRSA championship highlighted their adaptability and continued success in collegiate-level competition.

The 2009 NIRSA national title added to BYU's rich sports legacy, demonstrating that the Cougars could excel in a variety of athletic competitions, even at the club level.

IN 2009, BYU'S WOMEN'S volleyball team made history by advancing to the NCAA Final Four for the first time in the program's history. This achievement marked a major milestone, elevating BYU's women's volleyball team to elite status in collegiate volleyball. The team had an outstanding season, showcasing a combination of skill, teamwork, and determination that propelled them to the national stage.

Their appearance in the Final Four was a testament to the growing strength of the program, which has continued to be a dominant force in women's volleyball since then. It set the foundation for future success, with BYU consistently ranking among the top teams in the NCAA.

In 2009, BYU's women's volleyball team featured several standout players who were crucial to their historic run to the NCAA Final Four. Some of the top players included:

1. Lindsey Metcalf – A key player for BYU, Metcalf was known for her exceptional skills as an outside hitter. She earned All-American honors and was instrumental in the team's success throughout the season.
2. Kayla Walker – As a middle blocker, Walker played a crucial role in both defense and offense for BYU. Her performance was a significant factor in the team's deep run in the tournament.
3. Stephanie Ferrin – Ferrin, a versatile player, contributed significantly as an outside hitter. Her ability to perform under pressure was vital to the team's success in the postseason.
4. Jennifer Hamson – Although Hamson's impact was more pronounced in later years, she was a rising star in 2009 and began making her mark as a future standout for the program.

These players, along with their teammates and coaching staff, worked together to achieve the program's first Final Four appearance, marking a significant moment in BYU women's volleyball history.

2011 Jimmer Fredette's 52-point game

In 2011, Jimmer Fredette delivered one of the most electrifying performances in college basketball history, scoring 52 points in the Mountain West Conference (MWC) Tournament semifinals. His record-breaking game against New Mexico not only cemented his legacy as one of the greatest scorers in NCAA history but also set the stage for BYU's impressive run to the Sweet 16 in the NCAA Tournament. Fredette's performance became a defining moment in a season that captivated fans and brought national attention to both Fredette and the BYU basketball program.

Jimmer Fredette had already built a reputation as a prolific scorer and one of the top players in the nation by the time the 2010-2011 season reached the MWC Tournament. Throughout his senior season, Fredette put up incredible scoring numbers, often from well beyond the three-point line, and his ability to shoot from distance, drive to the basket, and score from any angle made him nearly impossible to guard. Fredette's offensive prowess earned him widespread admiration and the nickname "The Jimmer," a symbol of his unique and dynamic playing style.

Going into the MWC Tournament, BYU had enjoyed a strong season, finishing the regular season with a 28-3 record and earning a top seed in the conference tournament. However, the tournament semifinal matchup against New Mexico presented a tough challenge. Earlier in the season, New Mexico had handed BYU one of its few losses, and they boasted a physical defense that had previously disrupted Fredette's rhythm. In a high-stakes game with NCAA Tournament seeding on the line, Fredette knew he needed to rise to the occasion.

From the opening tip, Fredette took control of the game. He scored in a variety of ways, knocking down deep three-pointers, finishing at the rim, and hitting difficult mid-range shots. New Mexico threw multiple defenders at him, but nothing could slow him down. Fredette's range and quick release made him a threat from anywhere on the court, and he seemed unfazed by the defensive pressure.

As the game progressed, it became clear that Fredette was having a special night. His 52 points came on an efficient 22-of-37 shooting from the field, including 7-of-14 from beyond the arc. He also added 3-of-3 free throws. Fredette's scoring barrage not only helped BYU secure a 87-76 victory but also broke the MWC Tournament record for points in a game, a record that still stands today. His 52-point explosion was the highest single-game point total by any NCAA Division I player that season and one of the most memorable individual performances in college basketball history.

Fredette's performance in the MWC Tournament semifinals elevated his already high profile, and he went on to win several national Player of the Year awards, including the prestigious Naismith Award and Wooden Award. His stellar play carried BYU into the NCAA Tournament, where the Cougars made a run to the Sweet 16, their best showing in the tournament since 1981.

Fredette's ability to take over games with his scoring and leadership was a major reason for BYU's success that season. His impact on the game extended beyond his incredible scoring; he inspired teammates with his work ethic and ability to perform under pressure. His 52-point game became the highlight of an unforgettable season, one that brought BYU basketball to the national spotlight and established Fredette as one of the most iconic players in college basketball.

Jimmer Fredette's 52-point game in the 2011 MWC Tournament semifinals remains one of the greatest individual performances in the history of college basketball. It was a testament to his extraordinary talent and competitiveness, and it set the stage for BYU's deep NCAA Tournament run, where they reached the Sweet 16. Fredette's legacy as a BYU legend continues to endure, and his remarkable scoring display that night is a memory that BYU fans and college basketball enthusiasts will never forget.

2011 Road win vs SEC opponent

On September 3, 2011, BYU's football team achieved a dramatic victory over Ole Miss in a highly anticipated matchup. Here's a detailed look at that game:

2011 BYU vs. Ole Miss Game:

- Date: September 3, 2011

- Location: Vaught-Hemingway Stadium, Oxford, Mississippi

- Result: BYU 14, Ole Miss 13

Game Highlights:

- Dramatic Finish: The game was a closely contested battle, and the decisive moment came late in the fourth quarter. BYU's defense scored a crucial go-ahead touchdown with just 26 seconds left on the clock.

- Key Play: The winning touchdown was scored by BYU's defense, with Bronco Mendenhall's squad capitalizing on a critical turnover. Defensive back Kyle Van Noy returned a fumble for the game-winning score, sealing the 14-13 victory for the Cougars.

- Performance: The defense was a standout, as they were able to shut down Ole Miss's offense effectively throughout the game, and the crucial turnover play exemplified their resilience and ability to seize key moments.

Significance:

- Significant Win: The victory was notable as it came in an SEC stadium, showcasing BYU's ability to compete and win against teams from one of the strongest conferences in college football.

- Momentum: The win provided a strong start to BYU's 2011 season and highlighted the Cougars' defensive prowess and ability to execute under pressure.

THIS GAME REMAINS A memorable moment in BYU football history, demonstrating the team's capability to perform in high-stakes situations and secure a victory on the road in a challenging environment.

2011 BYU Women's cross country WCC championship

In 2011, the BYU women's cross country team achieved a significant milestone by winning the West Coast Conference (WCC) Championship. This victory marked a critical moment for the program and set the stage for a strong performance at the NCAA Championships.

Key Highlights of the 2011 Season:

1. WCC CHAMPIONSHIP Victory:

○ The BYU women's cross country team dominated the WCC Championship, securing the title with impressive individual and team performances. The championship was held on October 29, 2011, and the Cougars showcased their depth and talent throughout the race.

2. Outstanding Performances:

○ Several runners contributed to the team's success, with standout performances from athletes such as Megan Gaskins, who finished among the top runners in the championship. The team's collective effort was instrumental in clinching the title.

3. Strong NCAA Showing:

○ Following their WCC title, the Cougars qualified for the NCAA Championships, where they continued to demonstrate their prowess. At the national level, BYU finished in the top tier, reinforcing their status as a competitive program in women's cross country.

4. Coaching Success:

○ Head coach Patrick Shane played a vital role in the team's development and success. His coaching strategies and focus on teamwork contributed to the athletes' strong performances throughout the season.

5. Team Depth:

○ The Cougars showcased their depth during the season, with numerous runners consistently performing at a high level. This depth was key to their success in both the WCC Championship and the NCAA Championships.

6. Legacy and Impact:

○ The 2011 WCC Championship victory solidified BYU's place in women's cross country as a competitive force within the conference. The success of this season inspired future runners and contributed to the overall growth of the program.

7. Future Aspirations:

○ The achievements of the 2011 season set the stage for continued success in subsequent years, as the Cougars aimed to build upon their momentum in both conference and national competitions.

Conclusion:

THE BYU WOMEN'S CROSS country team's victory in the 2011 WCC Championship and their strong performance at the NCAA Championships highlighted the program's talent and dedication. This season not only marked a significant achievement for the athletes involved but also established a legacy of excellence for BYU women's cross country.

2011 BYU men's basketball Sweet 16

In 2011, the BYU men's basketball team faced a significant challenge when star player Brandon Davies was suspended late in the season. However, the Cougars rallied behind their leading scorer, Jimmer Fredette, and made an impressive run to the Sweet 16 of the NCAA Tournament.

Key Highlights of the 2011 Season:

1. BRANDON DAVIES' Suspension:

○ Brandon Davies, a key forward for the Cougars, was suspended in March 2011 due to a violation of team rules. His absence was a considerable blow to the team, as he was a vital contributor on both ends of the court.

2. Rise of Jimmer Fredette:

○ Jimmer Fredette stepped up as the focal point of the BYU offense. Known for his scoring ability and versatility, he took on an even larger role, leading the team with exceptional performances throughout the remainder of the season.

3. Strong Regular Season:

○ Prior to Davies' suspension, BYU had a successful regular season, finishing with a record of 26-8 and securing a strong seeding in the NCAA Tournament. The team had already established a reputation as a competitive force in college basketball.

4. NCAA Tournament Success:

○ Despite the setback of losing Davies, BYU entered the NCAA Tournament as a 3-seed. They won their opening game against Wofford and followed that with a notable victory over Gonzaga in the second round, showcasing their resilience and talent.

5. Sweet 16 Appearance:

○ The Cougars advanced to the Sweet 16, where they faced the Florida Gators. Although BYU ultimately lost the game, their journey to this stage was a testament to the team's determination and ability to adapt under pressure.

6. Impact of Fredette's Play:

○ Jimmer Fredette's outstanding performance during the tournament and the entire season earned him significant recognition, culminating in him winning the Naismith College Player of the Year award. He averaged over 28 points per game in the NCAA Tournament, leading the Cougars with his dynamic scoring.

7. Legacy of the 2011 Team:

○ The 2011 season is remembered for its resilience in the face of adversity. The Cougars' ability to rally after Davies' suspension and still make a deep tournament run elevated the program's profile and left a lasting impact on BYU basketball history.

8. Fan and Community Support:

○ The BYU community and fans rallied around the team, providing unwavering support during the tournament. The excitement surrounding Fredette and the team's success brought significant attention to BYU basketball.

The 2011 BYU men's basketball season is a remarkable story of resilience and teamwork. Despite the challenges posed by Brandon

Davies' suspension, the Cougars, led by Jimmer Fredette, made a strong run to the Sweet 16 in the NCAA Tournament. This season is celebrated for its memorable performances and the way the team came together to achieve success against the odds.

Brandon Davies, a talented forward for the BYU men's basketball team, faced a significant challenge in March 2011 when he was suspended due to a violation of the university's honor code. The suspension came just weeks before the NCAA Tournament, and it had a profound impact on the Cougars' season.

Key Details Surrounding Brandon Davies' Suspension:

1. REASON FOR SUSPENSION:

○ Davies was suspended for violating BYU's honor code, which governs conduct related to academic integrity and personal behavior. Specific details regarding the violation were not publicly disclosed, but it was confirmed that he breached the university's standards.

2. Impact on the Team:

○ His suspension was a significant blow to the BYU basketball team, as Davies was a key player averaging 11.1 points, 6.2 rebounds, and 1.5 blocks per game during the season. His absence created a void in the lineup and challenged the team's depth and cohesion.

3. Team Response:

○ Following Davies' suspension, the Cougars had to quickly adapt to his absence. Jimmer Fredette, the team's star player, elevated his game, leading the team through the NCAA Tournament. The Cougars showed remarkable resilience, making a strong run to the Sweet 16.

4. Public and Media Reaction:

○ The suspension garnered significant media attention, particularly because it occurred just before the NCAA Tournament. Many fans and commentators were concerned about how the team would fare without Davies, but BYU's strong performance, largely led by Fredette, helped mitigate some of the disappointment.

5. Aftermath and Davies' Future:

○ After the season concluded, Davies expressed his regret over the incident and acknowledged the importance of the university's honor code. He returned to play for BYU the following season after completing the necessary requirements set forth by the university.

6. Professional Career:

○ Following his time at BYU, Davies went on to pursue a professional basketball career. He went undrafted in the 2013 NBA Draft but signed with the Los Angeles D-Fenders (now known as the South Bay Lakers) in the NBA Development League (D-League). He later played overseas, including stints in leagues in Australia and Europe.

Conclusion:

BRANDON DAVIES' SUSPENSION in 2011 was a pivotal moment in BYU basketball history, as it tested the team's resilience during a crucial time. Despite the challenges, the Cougars showcased their talent and determination, ultimately achieving a memorable run in the NCAA Tournament. Davies' experience serves as a reminder of the importance of personal conduct and the standards upheld by institutions like BYU.

2012 Kyle Van Noy's Poinsettia Bowl

Kyle Van Noy's performance in the 2012 Poinsettia Bowl is often regarded as one of the most dominant defensive showings in college football bowl history. The BYU linebacker was instrumental in leading the Cougars to a 23-6 victory over San Diego State, largely thanks to his ability to make game-changing plays on defense.

Here's a breakdown of Van Noy's incredible performance:

- Two Defensive Touchdowns: Van Noy single-handedly scored two of BYU's three touchdowns. In the third quarter, with BYU trailing 6-3, Van Noy forced a fumble, recovered it, and returned it 17 yards for a touchdown to give BYU the lead. Later in the game, he intercepted a pass at San Diego State's 1-yard line and immediately returned it for his second touchdown.

- Stat Line: In addition to the two touchdowns, Van Noy had a sack, a forced fumble, a fumble recovery, an interception, and several tackles. His complete dominance on both the stat sheet and in game momentum earned him the Poinsettia Bowl Defensive MVP.

Van Noy's performance was crucial in turning what had been a tight, defensive struggle into a decisive win for BYU. It also solidified his reputation as one of the top defensive players in college football, and it is often remembered as one of the best individual defensive efforts in bowl history.

2012 BYU Women's soccer

The BYU women's soccer team's deepest run in the NCAA Tournament came in 2012 when they advanced to the Elite Eight. This marked one of the most successful seasons in program history under longtime head coach Jennifer Rockwood.

In the 2012 season:

- BYU finished with a record of 20-2-2, dominating their conference and earning a high seed in the NCAA Tournament.

- The team made it to the Elite Eight after defeating Marquette in the Sweet 16.

- In the Elite Eight, BYU faced North Carolina, one of the most storied programs in women's soccer. After a hard-fought match that ended in a 0-0 draw, BYU ultimately lost in a penalty shootout, falling just short of advancing to the College Cup (Final Four).

This 2012 run remains a defining moment for BYU women's soccer and one of the program's greatest accomplishments.

Throughout its history, BYU women's soccer has produced several standout players who have made significant contributions to the program. Some of the most notable players include:

1. Ashley Hatch (2013–2016)

- Position: Forward

- Accolades: Hatch was a star for BYU, earning All-American honors and leading the team in goals multiple seasons. She was a semifinalist for the Hermann Trophy (awarded to the top college player).

- Pro Career: Hatch was drafted second overall in the 2017 NWSL Draft and has since played for the Washington Spirit, earning NWSL Golden Boot in 2021 and representing the U.S. Women's National Team.

2. Michele Vasconcelos (née Murphy) (2013–2016)

- Position: Forward/Midfielder

- Accolades: Vasconcelos was a dynamic player known for her versatility and playmaking ability. She helped lead BYU to several strong seasons and earned All-WCC honors.

- Pro Career: She has played professionally in the NWSL, most notably for the Chicago Red Stars and Utah Royals.

3. Elise Flake (2016–2019)

- Position: Forward

- Accolades: Flake had an exceptional career at BYU, earning All-American honors and helping the Cougars make a deep run in the NCAA Tournament in 2019. She finished her senior season with 20 goals and was one of the nation's top scorers.

4. Katie Larkin (2005–2008)

- Position: Midfielder/Forward

● Accolades: Larkin was a three-time All-American and one of the best players in BYU history. She was known for her technical ability, vision, and leadership on the field.

● National Team Experience: Larkin also earned caps for the U.S. Women's National Team.

5. Alyssa Jefferson (2016–2019)

● Position: Defender

● Accolades: Jefferson was a key part of BYU's defense, earning All-WCC honors and helping the team achieve multiple shutouts. Her leadership and defensive prowess were vital to BYU's success in the 2019 NCAA Tournament.

THESE PLAYERS HELPED establish BYU as a top-tier women's soccer program, contributing to deep NCAA tournament runs and conference championships.

2014 BYU's women's volleyball makes national championship game

In 2014, BYU's women's volleyball team had an extraordinary run in the NCAA Women's Volleyball Championship, making history as the first unseeded team to reach the national championship match.

Here's a detailed look at their journey:

- **Final Four Semifinal:** BYU faced off against the No. 2 seed, the University of Texas, in the national semifinals. BYU stunned the Longhorns with a decisive 3-0 sweep (25-23, 25-16, 25-19), securing their spot in the championship match. This upset was one of the highlights of the tournament and solidified BYU's place as a major contender.

- **National Championship Match:** In the final, BYU faced Penn State, a perennial volleyball powerhouse. Despite their remarkable tournament run, BYU fell to Penn State 3-0 (21-25, 19-25, 14-25). Penn State's victory earned them their seventh national title, but BYU's achievement in reaching the final as an unseeded team remains a historic milestone in NCAA volleyball.

BYU's 2014 season was marked by strong team dynamics, skillful play, and a fighting spirit that earned them national recognition.

2014 Men's National Volleyball Championship

2014 Men's Volleyball National Championship:

- Date: May 3, 2014

- Location: Pauley Pavilion, Los Angeles, California

- Opponent: Loyola Chicago Ramblers

Match Highlights:

- Result: BYU won the championship match in four sets: 25-21, 25-21, 22-25, 25-19.

- Key Players:

○ Taylor Sander: The standout player and tournament MVP, Sander's exceptional performance throughout the match was crucial for BYU's success.

○ Fousseni Toure: Another significant contributor, Toure's all-around play was instrumental in securing the victory.

Coaching Staff:

- Shawn Olmstead: The head coach of BYU's men's volleyball team, Olmstead's leadership and strategic acumen were pivotal in guiding the team to the championship.

2015 game-winning Hail Mary against Nebraska

In 2015, BYU's season opener against Nebraska was a thrilling game, but it was not quarterback Taysom Hill who threw the game-winning Hail Mary. Instead, it was Tanner Mangum, Hill's backup, who stepped in after Hill was injured during the game and delivered the iconic play.

Here's how the dramatic game unfolded:

- Taysom Hill's Performance: Hill started the game and was having a strong showing, rushing for two touchdowns and keeping BYU competitive. However, in the third quarter, Hill suffered a season-ending foot injury, leaving the game with BYU trailing 28-27.

- Tanner Mangum's Hail Mary: Freshman Tanner Mangum replaced Hill and led BYU's final drive. With just one second left on the clock and BYU down 28-27, Mangum launched a 42-yard Hail Mary pass to wide receiver Mitch Mathews, who caught the ball in the end zone as time expired. The miraculous touchdown gave BYU a stunning 33-28 victory over Nebraska, ending the Cornhuskers' 29-year streak of winning home openers.

The game became an instant classic, and Mangum's Hail Mary pass is one of the most memorable moments in BYU football history. Although Taysom Hill's injury was a huge blow, the Cougars' resilience in the face of adversity made the 2015 season opener unforgettable.

In 2015, Bronco Mendenhall was the head coach of the BYU football team. He served as BYU's head coach from 2005 to 2015 and was known for his strong leadership and defensive coaching. Under Mendenhall, BYU enjoyed consistent success, including bowl appearances in each of his 11 seasons.

The 2015 season was Mendenhall's final year as BYU's head coach. After that season, he accepted the head coaching position at the University of Virginia. During his time at BYU, Mendenhall helped shape the program's identity and left a lasting legacy.

2016 BYU women's soccer WCC Title

In 2016, the BYU women's soccer team had a remarkable season, culminating in the capture of the West Coast Conference (WCC) title and a significant run in the NCAA Tournament. This season showcased the Cougars' talent, determination, and commitment to excellence.

Key Highlights of the 2016 Season:

1. WCC CHAMPIONSHIP:

○ The Cougars secured the WCC title, marking a significant achievement in the program's history. This victory highlighted their dominance in the conference and underscored their status as one of the top teams in women's soccer.

2. Regular Season Success:

○ BYU had an impressive regular season, finishing with a strong overall record. The team's success was built on a combination of solid defense, skilled midfield play, and a potent offense that produced numerous goals throughout the season.

3. NCAA Tournament Performance:

○ Following their conference championship, the Cougars earned a spot in the NCAA Tournament. They made a deep run, advancing to the later rounds of the tournament and showcasing their skill and resilience against formidable opponents.

4. Key Players:

○ The success of the 2016 team was driven by standout performances from several key players. Notable contributions came from both the offensive and defensive units, with players stepping up in crucial moments to secure victories.

5. Coaching Excellence:

○ Head coach Jennifer Rockwood played a pivotal role in guiding the team through the season. Her coaching philosophy and ability to develop talent contributed significantly to the Cougars' success and growth as a competitive program.

6. Fan Support:

○ The Cougars enjoyed strong support from their fans throughout the season, creating an energetic and passionate atmosphere at home games. The community's engagement helped foster a strong team spirit and morale.

7. Legacy and Impact:

○ The 2016 season reinforced BYU women's soccer as a prominent program within the WCC and nationally. Their performance not only elevated the program's profile but also inspired future generations of players to aspire to similar success.

Conclusion:

THE BYU WOMEN'S SOCCER team's triumph in capturing the WCC title and making a deep NCAA Tournament run in 2016 was a defining moment for the program. This season demonstrated the Cougars' commitment to excellence and their ability to compete at the highest levels, leaving a lasting impact on BYU women's soccer history.

2017 Ashley Hatch, NWSL Rookie of the Year

In 2017, Ashley Hatch, a former standout from BYU's women's soccer team, earned the NWSL Rookie of the Year award, marking an impressive start to her professional career. Hatch, who was drafted by the North Carolina Courage as the second overall pick in the 2017 NWSL Draft, quickly made an impact in her first season.

Known for her exceptional speed, scoring ability, and relentless work ethic, Hatch scored 7 goals in 24 appearances, helping her team finish at the top of the league standings. Her stellar performance not only highlighted her transition from collegiate soccer to the professional level but also confirmed her as one of the league's most promising young talents.

At BYU, Hatch had an illustrious career, finishing as one of the school's all-time top scorers. Her success in the NWSL Rookie of the Year award solidified her as a key player to watch in women's soccer and showcased her ability to thrive at both the collegiate and professional levels.

The former BYU Cougar scored twice in the Washington Spirits' 3-0 victory over the Houston Dash. Her second goal of the match was her 50th career goal. She is the seventh NWSL player to score 50 regular season goals, according to the Spirit.

2019 the BYU men's cross country team won NCAA national championship

In 2019, the BYU men's cross country team won its first-ever NCAA national championship, capping a historic season with a dominant performance at the national meet held in Terre Haute, Indiana. Under the leadership of head coach Ed Eyestone, a former BYU runner and two-time Olympian, the Cougars executed a near-perfect race, outpacing their top rivals and solidifying their place in history.

Key Details of the 2019 Championship Run:

- Team Score: BYU finished with 109 points, securing the national title ahead of Northern Arizona University (NAU), which finished with 163 points. NAU had been the defending champion and was heavily favored, but BYU's depth and strategy overwhelmed them on race day.

- Top Performers:

○ Conner Mantz: Mantz was the team's top finisher, placing 10th overall with a time of 30:40.0 in the 10K race. His aggressive pacing and strong finish were crucial for BYU's team score.

○ Casey Clinger: Clinger, who had returned from a two-year LDS mission, contributed significantly, finishing 29th with a time of 31:07.9.

○ Jacob Heslington, Daniel Carney, and Matt Owens rounded out the top five scorers for BYU, each delivering solid performances that helped secure the victory.

Team Depth and Strategy:

WHAT MADE BYU'S PERFORMANCE so impressive in 2019 was their exceptional depth. The Cougars didn't rely solely on one or two standout runners; instead, they used a pack-running strategy, with their top five scorers finishing within a span of 50 seconds of each other. This balanced approach allowed them to take control of the race early and maintain their advantage over key rivals like NAU and Colorado.

Historical Significance:

THE 2019 TITLE WAS BYU's first national championship in men's cross country, breaking a long-standing quest for the top prize. The Cougars had come close in previous years, consistently placing among the top teams at nationals, but 2019 was the year they finally reached the pinnacle of collegiate cross country.

For head coach Ed Eyestone, the victory was especially sweet. As a former NCAA individual cross country champion (1984), leading BYU to a team championship was a fulfillment of both personal and program goals.

This win further solidified BYU's reputation as one of the premier cross country programs in the country, not just for their 2019 title but for their consistent performances over the years.

2014 BYU Rugby Third Straight National Championship

In 2014, the BYU rugby team achieved a remarkable feat by winning the National Championship, further solidifying their reputation as a powerhouse in collegiate rugby. This victory was a significant moment for the program and highlighted the team's dedication and talent.

Key Highlights of the 2014 Season:

1. NATIONAL CHAMPIONSHIP Victory:

o The BYU rugby team secured the USA Rugby Division I-A National Championship, triumphing in the final match against Cal Poly. This victory marked BYU's third national title in the last four years, showcasing their dominance in collegiate rugby.

2. Strong Season Performance:

o Throughout the regular season, BYU demonstrated consistent excellence, finishing with a strong record. The team's depth and skill were evident in their performances, as they outplayed many formidable opponents.

3. Key Players:

o The team featured several standout players who contributed significantly to their success, including key performers who excelled in both offensive and defensive roles. Their teamwork and individual skills were instrumental in the championship run.

4. Coaching Excellence:

○ Head coach David Smyth played a crucial role in guiding the team. His strategic approach and ability to develop player skills contributed significantly to the Cougars' success throughout the season.

5. Championship Match Highlights:

○ In the championship match, BYU showcased their tactical prowess and physicality on the field. The team executed well-coordinated plays and maintained strong defensive strategies to secure their victory.

6. Legacy of Success:

○ The 2014 national title added to BYU rugby's storied history, reinforcing their status as a top contender in collegiate rugby. The team's achievements helped raise the profile of rugby at BYU and attracted attention to the program.

7. Impact on the Program:

○ Winning the national championship not only elevated the program's status but also inspired future generations of rugby players at BYU. The success served as a motivating factor for both current athletes and recruits looking to join the program.

8. Community and Fan Support:

○ The Cougars enjoyed strong support from fans and the local community throughout the season. The enthusiasm and backing of the fans created an energized atmosphere at home matches, contributing to the team's motivation.

Conclusion:

THE BYU RUGBY TEAM'S victory in the 2014 National Championship was a defining moment for the program, showcasing their talent, dedication, and competitive spirit. This achievement further established BYU as a powerhouse in collegiate rugby and left a lasting legacy for future teams to aspire to. The combination of skilled athletes, effective coaching, and community support played a crucial role in this remarkable season.

2014 BYU women's volleyball NCAA national championship game

In 2014, the BYU women's volleyball team made history by reaching the NCAA national championship game for the first time in the program's history. This remarkable achievement represented a significant milestone for the team and showcased their talent and determination on a national stage.

Key Highlights of the 2014 Season:

1. HISTORIC RUN:

○ The Cougars had an outstanding season, showcasing their skill and teamwork throughout the NCAA tournament. Their journey to the championship match captured the attention of fans and volleyball enthusiasts across the country.

2. Dominant Team Performance:

○ Led by head coach Heather Olmstead, BYU displayed a well-rounded and dominant performance throughout the season, finishing with a strong overall record. The team was known for its powerful offense and solid defense, making them a formidable opponent.

3. Key Players:

○ Star players, including Jennifer Hamson, who was a standout outside hitter, played a crucial role in the team's success. Hamson's exceptional athleticism and skill were instrumental in leading the Cougars through the tournament.

o Other key contributors included Alexa Gray and Mikayla McKenna, who provided crucial points and played vital roles in the team's overall success.

4. NCAA Tournament Journey:

o The Cougars navigated through a challenging NCAA tournament, defeating several highly ranked teams to reach the championship match. Their victories included impressive performances in the early rounds and the Final Four, where they defeated the University of Nebraska in a thrilling semifinal match.

5. National Championship Match:

o BYU faced Florida in the national championship match held in Tampa, Florida. The match was highly competitive, and both teams showcased their skills in front of a large audience. Although the Cougars fought valiantly, they ultimately lost to Florida in a closely contested match, finishing as the national runners-up.

6. Significance of the Achievement:

o Reaching the NCAA championship game marked a watershed moment for BYU women's volleyball, elevating the program's profile nationally and establishing it as a serious contender in collegiate volleyball. This success inspired future generations of players and heightened interest in the program.

7. Recognition and Awards:

o The Cougars received numerous accolades following their successful season, including recognition for individual players who earned All-American honors and conference awards. Their performance helped to solidify BYU's reputation as a top-tier volleyball program.

8. Impact on Future Seasons:

○ The success of the 2014 season laid a strong foundation for future teams. It increased recruitment interest from talented players and helped to foster a winning culture within the program.

Conclusion:

BYU WOMEN'S VOLLEYBALL reaching the 2014 NCAA national championship game was a historic achievement that showcased the program's growth and competitive spirit. The team's remarkable journey not only brought national recognition but also set the stage for continued success in subsequent seasons. The legacy of the 2014 team continues to inspire current players and serves as a proud moment in BYU athletics history.

2017 Ashley Hatch, NWSL Rookie of the Year

In 2017, Ashley Hatch, a former standout from BYU's women's soccer team, earned the NWSL Rookie of the Year award, marking an impressive start to her professional career. Hatch, who was drafted by the North Carolina Courage as the second overall pick in the 2017 NWSL Draft, quickly made an impact in her first season.

Known for her exceptional speed, scoring ability, and relentless work ethic, Hatch scored 7 goals in 24 appearances, helping her team finish at the top of the league standings. Her stellar performance not only highlighted her transition from collegiate soccer to the professional level but also confirmed her as one of the league's most promising young talents.

At BYU, Hatch had an illustrious career, finishing as one of the school's all-time top scorers. Her success in the NWSL Rookie of the Year award solidified her as a key player to watch in women's soccer and showcased her ability to thrive at both the collegiate and professional levels.

The former BYU Cougar scored twice in the Washington Spirits' 3-0 victory over the Houston Dash. Her second goal of the match was her 50th career goal. She is the seventh NWSL player to score 50 regular season goals, according to the Spirit.

2021 BYU joins Big 12

BYU's inclusion in the Big 12 Conference in 2021 was a historic and significant moment for the program. Here's a summary of that pivotal change:

Key Points about BYU Joining the Big 12:

1. Historic Move: After being an independent program since 2011, BYU joined the Big 12 Conference, marking a major shift in its athletic and football programs. This move represented a significant step forward in terms of national exposure and competition.

2. Membership Start: BYU officially became a member of the Big 12 Conference on July 1, 2023. The Cougars joined the conference alongside other new members, including Cincinnati, Houston, and UCF.

3. Impact on Program:

○ Increased Exposure: Joining the Big 12 provided BYU with more national television coverage and increased visibility, which is beneficial for recruiting and program growth.

○ Competitive Schedule: The Big 12 is known for its competitive football programs, and joining the conference meant that BYU would face a higher level of competition regularly.

4. Previous Independent Status: Before joining the Big 12, BYU had been an independent program in football since leaving the Mountain West Conference in 2011. During that time, the Cougars enjoyed a successful run, including notable bowl appearances and a strong national presence.

5. Football Program Growth: Joining the Big 12 was part of BYU's broader efforts to align with a Power Five conference and enhance its athletic and academic standing on a national scale.

THIS MOVE WAS A LANDMARK event for BYU football and the university's athletic department, as it marked the beginning of a new era of competition and opportunity for the program.